MW00904869

light & easy
desserts

Chef
express

Published by:
TRIDENT REFERENCE PUBLISHING
801 12th Avenue South, Suite 400
Naples, Fl 34102 USA

Tel: + 1 (239) 649-7077
www.tridentreference.com
email: sales@tridentreference.com

light & easy
desserts

Light and Easy Desserts
© TRIDENT REFERENCE PUBLISHING

Publisher
Simon St. John Bailey

Editor-in-chief
Susan Knightley

Prepress
Precision Prep & Press

All rights reserved. No part of this book may
be stored, reproduced or transmitted in any
form and by any means without written
permission of the Publisher, except in the
case of brief quotations embodied in critical
articles and reviews.

Includes Index
ISBN 1582796823
UPC 6 15269 96823 9

Printed in The United States

introduction

There are a lot of us who think that a meal without dessert is not complete. We share that opinion, but are aware that those delights that gratify us so much can provide undesired calories and generate reproaches from the body for not staying in shape, if these are not properly selected. Furthermore, we know that,

light and easy desserts
introduction

while the palate demands its sweet quota at the end of the menu, the stomach asks us not to overload it, as it already has quite a lot of work with the savory dishes.

How to conciliate so many opposite desires? With the exquisite dessert selection we present in this book. There are unmissable findings as they could be qualified as light both for their consistency and their relatively reduced caloric value.

- Fresh fruit is the irreplaceable basis. They provide not only color and flavor, but also necessary vitamins for a good nutrition. During the past decades, the tropical and exotic fruit availability has revolutioned the art of dessert making. In the big supermarkets, pineapple, papaya and mango are not rarities anymore, and in the gourmet boutiques you can easily find chirimoyas and star fruits.

- It is not indispensable to eliminate egg yolks, cream, or butter completely, but it is important to use them moderately.

- Thanks to the industry development, dairy products are not forbidden anymore. Light cream and low-fat yogurt are good allies that provide smoothness and greasiness. Nonfat sour cream is ideal for ice-cream, and low-fat unsalted cream cheese or cottage cheese can be used in place of ricotta cheese.

- Egg whites, rich in proteins, enable you to create airy textures. Gelatin, which has practically no calories, provides firmness to the molded desserts. Both contribute to reduce the fat content in the mixtures.

- Spices corroborate that a pinch makes the difference. Vanilla, cinnamon, anise, saffron, nutmeg, cloves and ginger rivalize against mint and citrus grated rind broadening the variety of tastes.

- Nuts add their crunchy note and wine, champagne, liqueurs and brandy show water is not the only liquid one may turn to. Even the most unconventional ingredients, such as pumpkin and tea, are main characters of this book's recipes.

Difficulty scale

■□□ I Easy to do

■■□ I Requires attention

■■■ I Requires experience

drunken
summer fruits

■□□ I Cooking time: 0 minute - Preparation time: 10 minutes

ingredients
> **375 g/12½ oz mixed berries (raspberries, blueberries, strawberries)**
> **2 white peaches, quartered**
> **2 nectarines, quartered**
> **¾ cup/185 ml/6 fl oz dessert wine**
> **2 tablespoons lime juice**

method
1. Place berries, peaches and nectarines in a bowl.
2. Pour wine and lime juice over fruit and toss gently to combine. Cover and chill for 20-30 minutes.
3. Serve in deep bowls with some of the marinade.

....

Serves 4-6

tip from the chef
When available, fresh apricots are a tasty addition to this summer dessert.

cream-topped
fruit

■□□ | Cooking time: 5 minutes - Preparation time: 10 minutes

method

1. Place sugar in a saucepan. Pour just enough water over sugar to cover. Boil until it forms a golden caramel; do not stir.
2. Meanwhile, arrange fruit on a serving bowl. Top with cream and pour caramel over the top just before serving.

....

Serves 4

ingredients

> 1 cup caster sugar
> 3 tablespoons water
> 1 cup papaya, peeled, seeded and cut into 2 cm/3/4 in cubes
> 4 kiwi fruits, peeled and cut into 2 cm/3/4 in cubes
> 1/2 cup strawberries, hulled
> 4 tablespoons whipped cream

tip from the chef

Raspberry coulis is a colorful alternative to caramel. To make coulis, blend or process fresh raspberries with a little icing sugar and a dash lemon juice, then push through a sieve to discard seeds.

lychee and
rockmelon salad

■□□ | Cooking time: 0 minute - Preparation time: 10 minutes

ingredients
> **1 rockmelon**
> **2 cups canned lychees, drained**
> **2 tablespoons freshly chopped mint**
> **3/4 cup sweet white wine**

method
1. Peel and seed rockmelon, cut flesh into cubes.
2. In a large bowl combine rockmelon, lychees and mint.
3. Pour over wine, toss well and refrigerate until ready to serve.

....
Serves 8

tip from the chef
Lychees are a rare subtropical fruit originating in South China. There the lychee is very important in their culture and is famed as "the king of fruit".

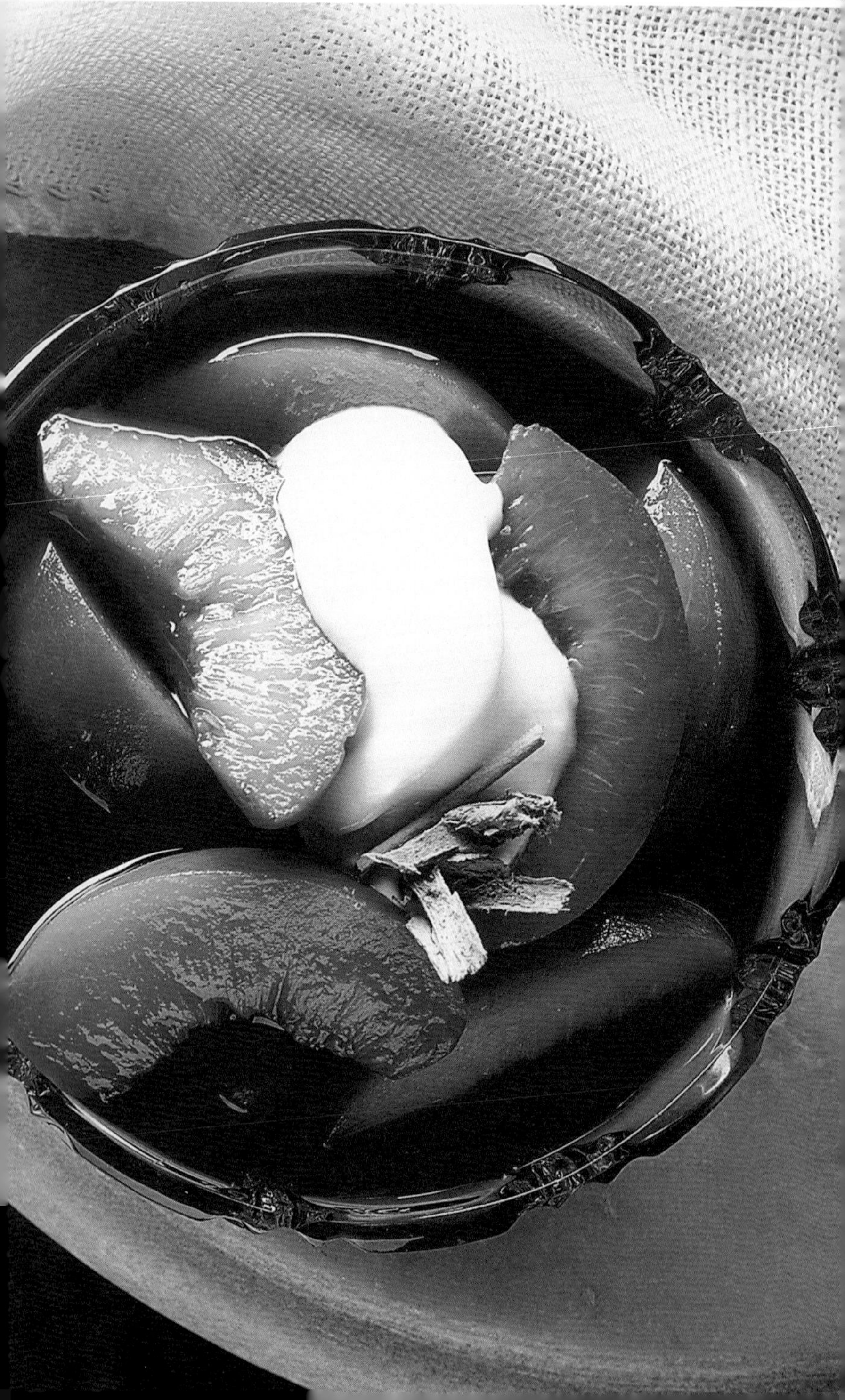

wine
compote

■□□ | Cooking time: 15 minutes - Preparation time: 10 minutes

method
1. Cut peaches into thick slices.
2. Place wine, honey and cinnamon stick into a saucepan and bring to the boil, reduce heat and simmer for 5 minutes.
3. Add peaches to saucepan and cook for 5-10 minutes or until slightly softened. Set aside to cool, then chill.

ingredients
> 6 firm ripe peaches, halved and stones removed
> 1 cup/250 ml/8 fl oz red wine
> 2-3 tablespoons honey
> 1 cinnamon stick

Serves 4

tip from the chef
As a serving suggestion, accompany with natural yogurt.

saffron-poached
pears

■□□ | Cooking time: 25 minutes - Preparation time: 10 minutes

ingredients
> **3/4 cup/185 g/6 oz sugar**
> **2 cinnamon sticks**
> **2 star anise**
> **1/4 teaspoon saffron threads**
> **8 cups/2 liters/3 1/2 pt water**
> **8 pears, peeled**

method
1. Combine sugar, cinnamon sticks, star anise, saffron and water in a large saucepan. Add pears, place over a low heat and bring to simmering. Simmer for 25 minutes or until pears are soft. Remove pan from heat and stand for 30 minutes.
2. To serve, place pears in shallow dessert bowls and spoon over poaching liquid.

....
Serves 8

tip from the chef
Serve this pretty dessert with thin sweet biscuits or almond bread. It can be prepared up to 3 hours in advance, however, the flavor will be best if it is not refrigerated prior to serving.

italian
stuffed peaches

■□□ | Cooking time: 25 minutes - Preparation time: 15 minutes

method

1. Cut peaches in half, peel and stone them (a).
2. In a small bowl, combine almonds, macaroons, sugar and butter, mix well (b).
3. Fill each of the peach halves with almond macaroon topping and place in a well greased baking tray (c).
4. Bake peaches in a moderate oven for 25 minutes.

Serves 6

ingredients

> **6 large slip-stone peaches**
> **$^1/_4$ cup blanched almonds**
> **$^1/_2$ cup crumbled macaroons**
> **3 tablespoons caster sugar**
> **4 tablespoons melted butter**

tip from the chef

These are also great for the barbecue. Wrap each filled peach half in aluminum foil and grill for 25 minutes. Serve warm.

a

b

c

apricots
with pear purée

■□□ I Cooking time: 10 minutes - Preparation time: 15 minutes

ingredients

- > **12 firm apricots, peeled**
- > **1/2 cup/120 g/4 oz caster sugar**
- > **1 teaspoon ground cinnamon**
- > **1 teaspoon ground nutmeg**
- > **1/2 teaspoon ground cloves**
- > **1 1/2 cups canned pear halves, drained and chopped**
- > **2 tablespoons freshly squeezed lemon juice**
- > **2 tablespoons freshly squeezed orange juice**
- > **1 tablespoon finely chopped fresh mint**
- > **cinnamon sticks, to decorate**

method

1. Place peeled apricots in a saucepan with enough water to cover. Add sugar, cinnamon, nutmeg and cloves (a), simmer until tender, about 10 minutes. Cool in syrup.
2. Blend or process pears with lemon and orange juice until smooth (b), stir in mint (c).
3. Spoon some pear purée into the bottom of each plate, arrange the poached apricots in each plate on the purée and decorate with the cinnamon sticks.

....
Serves 4

tip from the chef

Spices are the magic touch for this simple dessert. You may like to try ginger instead of cloves.

a

b

c

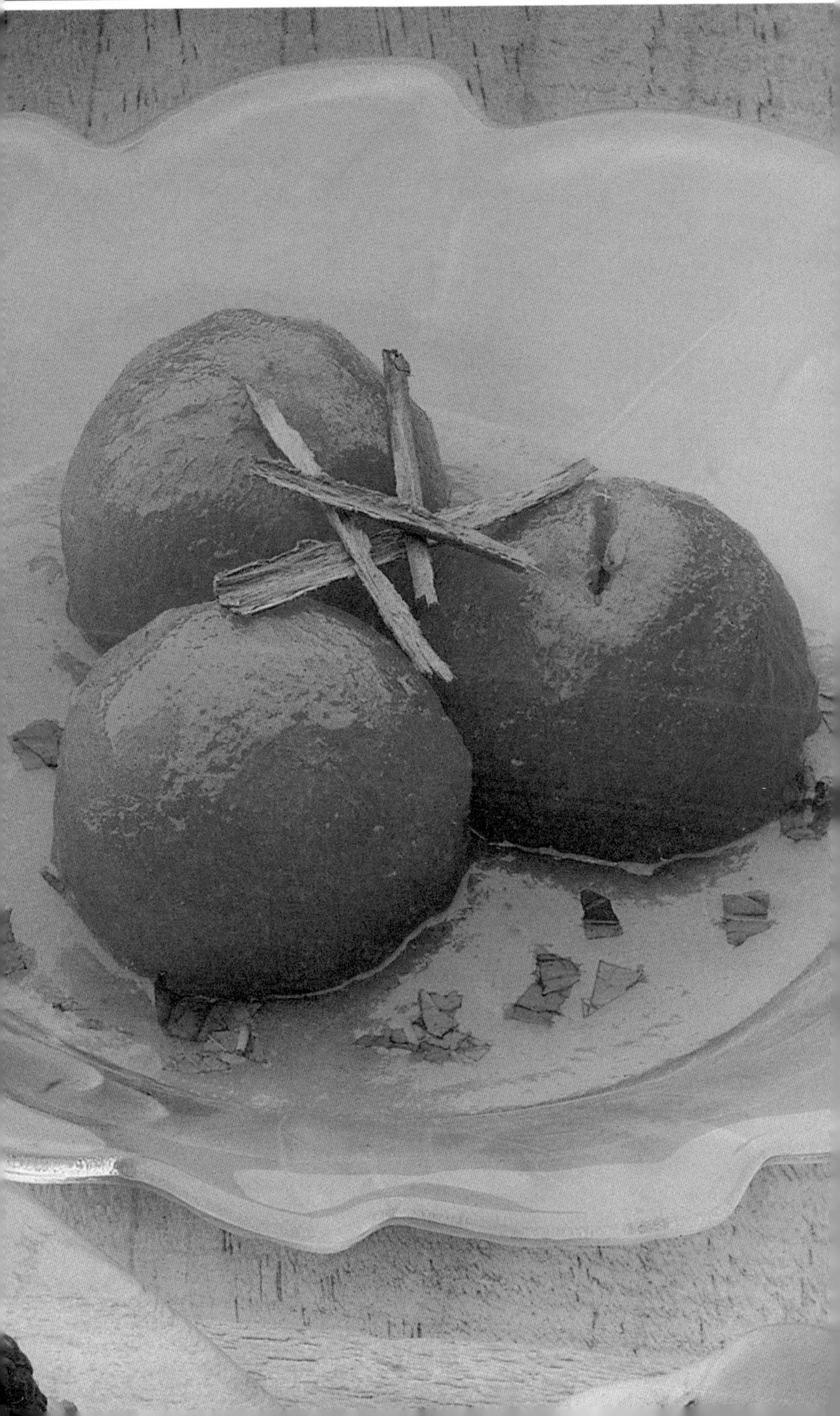

peaches
with custard

| Cooking time: 35 minutes - Preparation time: 20 minutes

method

1. Place peach halves cut side down in an ovenproof dish. Evenly pour over Amaretto, sprinkle sugar over the top and bake in a moderate oven for 30 minutes.
2. Heat berries with brown sugar and 2 tablespoons water in a medium saucepan until simmering. Remove from heat, push through a sieve and discard any pips or skin. Chill purée.
3. Mix custard, cream and brandy together until combined. Spoon a puddle of custard into the base of each serving plate. Using a teaspoon, drop small dots of purée, 2 cm/3/4 in apart, around the edge of custard. Run a skewer through the center of each dot, pulling continuously through the custard until all the dots are shaped into hearts.
4. Place two baked peach halves in the center of each custard puddle, spoon a little of the Amaretto syrup over peaches and decorate with mint.

ingredients

> 4 peaches, halved, stoned and peeled
> 3/4 cup/185 ml/6 fl oz Amaretto liqueur
> 1/2 cup/120 g/4 oz caster sugar
> 1 cup berries (blackberries, raspberries, blueberries)
> 3 tablespoons brown sugar
> 1 cup/250 ml/8 fl oz carton custard
> 1/2 cup/125 ml/4 fl oz light cream
> 2 teaspoons brandy
> mint to garnish

....
Serves 4

tip from the chef

Cointreau or another orange flavored liqueur can be used instead of Amaretto.

summer
puddings

■■□ | Cooking time: 5 minutes - Preparation time: 25 minutes

ingredients
> ½ cup/120 g/4 oz caster sugar
> 2 cups/500 ml/16 fl oz water
> 875 g/1¾ lb mixed berries (raspberries, strawberries, blueberries, blackberries)
> 14 slices bread, crusts removed

berry sauce
> 155 g/5 oz mixed berries
> 2 tablespoons icing sugar
> 1 tablespoon fresh lemon juice
> 2 tablespoons water

tip from the chef
Fresh or frozen berries can be used to make this dessert. Garnish with additional berries.

method
1. Place sugar and water in a saucepan and cook over a low heat, stirring, until sugar dissolves. Bring to the boil, reduce heat, add berries and simmer for 4-5 minutes or until fruit is soft, but still retains its shape. Drain, reserving liquid (a), and cool.
2. Cut 8 circles of bread (b). Line the base of four ½ cup/125 ml/4 fl oz capacity ramekins with 4 of the bread circles. Cut remaining bread slices into fingers and line the sides of ramekins. Spoon fruit into ramekins (c) and pour enough reserved liquid to moisten bread well, then cover with remaining bread circles. Reserve any remaining liquid. Cover ramekins with aluminum foil, top with a weight, and refrigerate overnight.
3. To make sauce, process berries, icing sugar, lemon juice and water until puréed. Push mixture through a sieve to remove seeds and chill until required.
4. Turn puddings onto individual serving plates, spoon sauce over or pass separately.

....
Serves 4

a

b

c

a

b

sugar-crusted
fruit baskets

■■■ | Cooking time: 25 minutes - Preparation time: 30 minutes

method

1. To make baskets, cut each pastry sheet crosswise into 8 cm/3^1/$_2$ in wide strips (a). Grease outsides of 4 small, round-based ramekins and place upside down on a greased baking tray. Brush pastry strips with butter and lay over ramekins, overlapping each strip, and bringing ends down to lay flat on tray (b). Brush again with butter and sprinkle generously with sugar. Bake at 200°C/400°F/Gas 6 for 10-15 minutes or until baskets are crisp and golden.

2. To poach fruit, place sugar, water and wine in a saucepan and cook over a low heat, stirring, until sugar dissolves. Add apricots, peaches, plums and nectarines to syrup and simmer for 3-4 minutes or until fruit is just soft. Remove saucepan from heat, stir in strawberries and set aside to stand for 5 minutes. Drain.

3. To make cream, push raspberry purée through a sieve to remove seeds. Place cream in a bowl, fold in icing sugar and purée.

4. Just prior to serving, place baskets on individual serving plates, fill with fruits and top with raspberry cream.

ingredients

sugar-crusted baskets
> 6 sheets filo pastry
> 60 g/2 oz butter, melted
> ^{1}/$_2$ cup/120 g/4 oz sugar

poached fruit
> 1 cup/250 g/8 oz sugar
> 1 cup/250 ml/8 fl oz water
> ^{1}/$_2$ cup/125 ml/4 fl oz white wine
> 4 apricots, stoned and quartered
> 4 peaches, stoned and cut into eighths
> 4 plums, stoned and quartered
> 4 nectarines, stoned and cut into eighths
> 16 strawberries

raspberry cream
> 125 g/4 oz raspberries, puréed
> ^{3}/$_4$ cup/185 ml/6 fl oz cream
> 4 teaspoons icing sugar

....
Serves 6

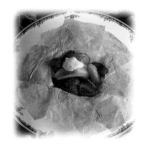

tip from the chef
Baskets are ideal for entertaining as each part can be made ahead of time. Leave the final assembly until just before serving or the fruit will cause the baskets to go soggy.

rhubarb fool

■■□ | Cooking time: 20 minutes - Preparation time: 20 minutes

ingredients

> **750 g/1¹/2 lb rhubarb, trimmed and cut into 1 cm/¹/2 in pieces**
> **1 cup/250 g/8 oz brown sugar**
> **¹/4 teaspoon ground cloves**
> **¹/2 teaspoon vanilla essence**
> **2 tablespoons lemon juice**
> **2 tablespoons orange juice**
> **¹/2 cup/100 g/3¹/2 oz cream**
> **³/4 cup/185 ml/6 fl oz natural yogurt**

method

1. Place rhubarb, sugar, cloves, vanilla essence and lemon and orange juices in a saucepan. Bring to the boil, then reduce heat and simmer, stirring occasionally, for 15 minutes or until rhubarb is soft and mixture thick. Spoon rhubarb mixture into a bowl, cover and chill.
2. Place cream in a bowl and beat until soft peaks form. Fold yogurt into cream, then fold in chilled rhubarb mixture to give a marbled effect. Spoon into individual serving glasses and chill.

....
Serves 8

tip from the chef

If you want to serve homemade orange biscuits with this refreshing dessert, beat 75 g/2¹/2 oz butter and 60 g/2 oz sugar until creamy, add 1 egg and 2 teaspoons grated orange rind and 90 g/3 oz flour and mix well. Place teaspoons of mixture on a baking tray and bake for 10 minutes or until golden.

pumpkin
mousse

■■□ | Cooking time: 0 minute - Preparation time: 20 minutes

method

1. Sprinkle gelatin over cold water and soften for 5 minutes. Add boiling water and mix well. Stir in cream, sugar, nutmeg, vanilla and ginger. Add lemon juice and pumpkin purée, mix until well combined. Refrigerate mixture for 10-15 minutes.
2. Beat egg whites with extra sugar until soft peaks form. Whisk pumpkin mixture for 10 seconds and fold in egg whites. Spoon into serving glasses, refrigerate before serving.

Serves 4-6

ingredients

> 3 teaspoons gelatin
> 4 tablespoons cold water
> 4 tablespoons boiling water
> 1/2 cup/125 ml/4 fl oz light cream
> 1/4 cup/60 g/2 oz caster sugar
> 1/2 teaspoon ground nutmeg
> 2 teaspoons vanilla essence
> 1 teaspoons ground ginger
> 2 tablespoons freshly squeezed lemon juice
> 1 cup pumpkin, cooked and puréed
> 4 egg whites
> 1 teaspoon caster sugar, extra

tip from the chef

Garnish with chocolate shavings and dust with icing sugar.

colorful
glasses

■□□ | Cooking time: 5 minutes - Preparation time: 20 minutes

ingredients

> 1/3 cup/90 ml/3 fl oz
  white wine
> 1 tablespoon lime juice
> 1/4 cup/60 g/2 oz sugar
> 1 1/4 cups/310 ml/10 fl oz
  light cream
> 1/3 cup/90 ml/3 fl oz
  mango purée
> 250 g/8 oz strawberries,
  hulled and sliced
> 2 kiwi fruits, peeled and
  chopped
> 1 mango, peeled and
  thinly sliced

method

1. Place wine, lime juice and sugar in a saucepan and cook over a medium heat, stirring constantly, until sugar dissolves. Remove from heat and set aside to cool. Refrigerate until chilled.
2. Place cream, mango purée and wine mixture in a large mixing bowl and beat until soft peaks form.
3. Arrange a layer of mango slices in the base of 4 dessert glasses and top with a spoonful of mango cream. Continue layering using kiwi fruits, strawberries and mango cream, finishing with mango cream. Refrigerate until required.

....
Serves 6

tip from the chef

Transparent glasses are ideal to serve layered desserts like this one, as the different colors of fruit and cream look very attractive.

fig trifle

■■□ | Cooking time: 5 minutes - Preparation time: 20 minutes

method

1. Cut sponge into small cubes, blend or process until crumbled. Sprinkle with Amaretto and set aside.
2. Combine caster sugar, water, Cassis and redcurrant jelly in a small saucepan over moderate heat. Bring to the boil, reduce heat and simmer for 3 minutes.
3. Place fig slices into a bowl, pour over redcurrant syrup and set aside to cool.
4. Arrange fig slices in the bottom of 4 dessert glasses, pour over a little syrup. Combine custard and cream, pour over figs. Top with soaked crumbs, chill before serving.

ingredients

> 1 packed sponge cake
> 2 tablespoons Amaretto liqueur
> 1 cup/250 g/8 oz caster sugar
> 1 cup/250 ml/8 fl oz water
> 2 tablespoons Cassis liqueur
> 3 tablespoons redcurrant jelly
> 10 fresh figs, sliced
> 1 cup carton custard
> 3/4 cup/185 ml/6 fl oz light cream

Serves 4

tip from the chef

Both Amaretto and Cassis liqueurs enhance the flavor of this smart easy dessert.

ricotta
custard

■□□ | Cooking time: 0 minute - Preparation time: 15 minutes

ingredients
> **4 sponge finger biscuits**
> **1/4 cup/60 ml/2 fl oz Amaretto liqueur**
> **4 eggs**
> **1/2 cup/120 g/4 oz caster sugar**
> **200 g/6 1/2 oz ricotta cheese**
> **2 teaspoons vanilla essence**
> **1/4 cup/40 g/1 1/4 oz icing sugar**

method
1. Place a sponge finger biscuit in each serving glass. Drizzle Amaretto over each biscuit.
2. Beat eggs with caster sugar until light and fluffy. Blend or process ricotta cheese with vanilla essence and icing sugar until smooth. Spoon ricotta mixture into egg mixture and beat until well combined.
3. Divide custard between the serving glasses and chill for 30 minutes before serving.

....
Serves 4

tip from the chef
You can sprinkle a few toasted almonds over the top of custard to add a crunchy touch.

passion
fruit bavarois

■■□ | Cooking time: 10 minutes - Preparation time: 15 minutes

ingredients

> ¹/4 cup/60 g/2 oz caster sugar
> 2 tablespoons Marsala or dry sherry
> 2 egg yolks
> 2 teaspoons gelatin
> 1 tablespoon boiling water
> 1 egg white
> ¹/4 cup/60 ml/2 fl oz cream, whipped
> ¹/4 cup/60 ml/2 fl oz passion fruit pulp

method

1. Place sugar, Marsala or sherry and egg yolks in a heatproof bowl set over a saucepan of simmering water. Cook, beating, for 8 minutes or until mixture is thick and leaves a ribbon trail when beaters are lifted from the mixture.
2. Dissolve gelatin in boiling water. Whisk gelatin mixture into custard mixture and set aside to cool.
3. Place egg white in a separate bowl and beat until stiff peaks form. Fold egg white mixture, cream and passion fruit pulp into custard.
4. Spoon mixture into 8 oiled small molds and refrigerate for 3 hours or until set. Unmold and garnish with extra passion fruit pulp.

....
Serves 8

tip from the chef

This dessert can be made the day before and stored, covered, in the refrigerator.

strawberry timbales

■□□ | Cooking time: 5 minutes - Preparation time: 15 minutes

method

1. Sprinkle gelatin over water in a cup and allow to soften for 5 minutes. Blend or process strawberries (reserving 2 for garnish) until smooth. Push purée through a sieve and pour into a small saucepan.

2. Stir in sugar and softened gelatin (a), cook purée over moderate heat for 3 minutes, stirring constantly. Transfer to a bowl.

3. Add yogurt and lime juice, mix well (b). Pour mixture into 4 fluted timbale molds (c) and refrigerate until set.

4. Beat cream with almond essence and icing sugar until just thickened. Ease timbales onto serving plates and serve with almond cream. Garnish with reserved strawberries and blanched almonds.

ingredients

> **3 teaspoons gelatin**
> **2 tablespoons water**
> **155 g/5 oz strawberries, hulled**
> **1/4 cup/60 g/2 oz caster sugar**
> **1 cup natural yogurt**
> **1 1/2 tablespoons freshly squeezed lime juice**
> **1/2 cup/125 ml/4 fl oz cream**
> **1 tablespoon almond essence**
> **1 tablespoon icing sugar**

....
Serves 4

tip from the chef

Moistening the interior part of the molds with water before filling with the mixture helps to unmold the timbales more easily.

a

b

c

coconut and
lime bavarois

■□□ I Cooking time: 8 minutes - Preparation time: 5 minutes

ingredients

> **2 cups/500 ml/16 fl oz light cream**
> **3/4 cup/125 g/4 oz icing sugar**
> **1 cup/250 ml/8 fl oz coconut milk**
> **3 teaspoons gelatin**
> **1/4 cup/60 ml/2 fl oz hot water**
> **1 tablespoon lime juice**
> **toasted coconut**

method

1. Place cream and icing sugar in a saucepan over a medium heat and bring to the boil. Cool slightly, then stir in coconut milk.
2. Sprinkle gelatin over hot water, stir to dissolve and cool to the same temperature as the cream mixture. Stir gelatin mixture and lime juice into cream mixture.
3. Divide mixture between six 3/4 cup/185 ml/ 6 fl oz capacity ramekins and chill for 3-4 hours or until set. Just prior to serving, turn out and sprinkle with toasted coconut.

....
Serves 6

tip from the chef

Coconut can be quickly and easily toasted in the microwave. Simply place 1/2 cup/ 45 g/1 1/2 oz desiccated coconut on a microwavable ceramic or glass plate and cook on High (100%) for 1 minute, stir, then continue cooking and stirring at 30-60 second intervals until coconut is evenly golden. The time it takes to toast coconut in this way depends on the moisture content of the coconut – watch carefully and check frequently as the coconut can burn quickly.

apricot mold

■□□ I Cooking time: 2 minutes - Preparation time: 10 minutes

method

1. Blend or process apricots until quite smooth.
2. Dissolve gelatin in apricot nectar in a heatproof bowl over a saucepan of simmering water. Stir into apricot purée.
3. Whip cream until thick and fold into apricot mixture.
4. Pour into four lightly oiled 1/2-cup capacity molds and refrigerate until set. Serve with fresh apricot slices, whipped cream and pistachios.

ingredients

> 8 apricots, stoned and chopped
> 3 teaspoons gelatin
> 1/4 cup/60 ml/2 fl oz apricot nectar
> 1 cup/250 ml/8 fl oz cream
> 2 apricots, extra, to decorate
> cream to serve
> 1/4 cup pistachios to serve

Serves 4

tip from the chef

This dessert becomes even lighter if unsalted low-fat cream cheese is used in place of cream.

ricotta hearts
with coulis

■■☐ | Cooking time: 5 minutes - Preparation time: 20 minutes

ingredients

> **1/3 cup cream cheese**
> **1/2 cup natural yogurt**
> **1 cup ricotta cheese**
> **2 tablespoons vanilla essence**
> **2 egg whites**
> **1/4 cup/40 g/11/4 oz icing sugar**
> **11/4 cups redcurrants or raspberries**
> **1/4 cup water**
> **1/4 cup/60 g/2 oz caster sugar**

method

1. Blend or process cream cheese with yogurt, ricotta cheese and vanilla until smooth.
2. Beat egg whites until fluffy. Gradually add icing sugar while motor is operating, beat until mixture is thick and glossy. Fold egg mixture into cheese mixture.
3. Lightly grease four 1/2-cup capacity heart-shaped molds. Carefully line with damp muslin. Spoon in mixture, make sure to fill all corners. Place in a tray and refrigerate for 4 hours until set.
4. Place redcurrants or raspberries in a small saucepan over moderate heat, add water and caster sugar, bring to the boil, reduce heat and simmer for 3 minutes. Push mixture through a sieve and chill coulis until ready to serve.
5. Turn out molds, remove muslin and pour a little coulis over mold.

....
Serves 4

tip from the chef

Garnish with some extra redcurrants if desired.

tea bavarois with berries

■ ■ □ | Cooking time: 15 minutes - Preparation time: 20 minutes

method

1. Place tea and milk in a medium saucepan over moderate heat and bring to just below boiling point. Beat egg yolks and sugar together with an electric mixer until thick and creamy.

2. Remove milk and tea mixture from heat and slowly strain into egg mixture while motor is running; discard tea leaves. Return mixture to saucepan and stir constantly over a low heat until custard thickens.

3. Dissolve gelatin in hot water, whisk into custard mixture and set aside to cool to room temperature, stirring occasionally. Whip cream until fluffy and fold into cold custard.

4. Lightly oil six $1/2$-cup capacity bavarois molds; pour mixture to the top, cover and refrigerate until ready to serve. To serve, turn out bavarois on dessert plates. Serve with blueberries.

ingredients

> **4 tablespoons breakfast tea**
> **2 cups/500 ml/16 fl oz milk**
> **6 egg yolks**
> **100 g/3$1/2$ oz caster sugar**
> **3 teaspoons gelatin**
> **$1/4$ cup/60 ml/2 fl oz very hot water**
> **$3/4$ cup/185 ml/6 oz light cream**
> **2 cups blueberries**

....
Serves 6

tip from the chef

Decorate with icing sugar and a sprig of fresh mint.

chilled passion fruit soufflé

■■□ | Cooking time: 10 minutes - Preparation time: 15 minutes

ingredients

> 4 tablespoons cornflour
> 3 cups/750 ml/1¼ pt milk
> ½ cup/120 g/4 oz caster sugar
> 2 teaspoons vanilla essence
> 3 teaspoons gelatin
> 5 tablespoons cold water
> ½ cup/125ml/4 fl oz cream
> 170 g/5½ oz canned passion fruit pulp
> ½ cup toasted coconut

method

1. In a small bowl, mix cornflour with 3 tablespoonfuls of the milk to form a paste. In a medium saucepan over moderate heat, slowly bring remaining milk, sugar, vanilla essence and cornflour paste to the boil, stirring constantly until mixture thickens. Remove from heat and cool to room temperature.

2. Dissolve gelatin in cold water, over a saucepan of simmering water, until clear. Whisk gelatin, cream and passion fruit pulp into the cooled custard and refrigerate for 10 minutes or until mixture is just beginning to set.

3. Grease four 1-cup capacity soufflé dishes and make a collar out of foil, extending 3 cm/1¼ in above the height of each soufflé dish. Pour mixture into prepared dishes, enough to rise 1cm/ ½ in above the dish rim.

4. Refrigerate soufflés for 2-3 hours or until set. To serve, remove the collars and gently turn the soufflés on their side and roll the exposed edge in coconut.

....
Serves 4

tip from the chef

The passion fruit is native of tropical America and was noted by the Europeans in Brazil in the 1500's.

ruby grapefruit sorbet

■□□ | Cooking time: 5 minutes - Preparation time: 10 minutes

method

1. Place sugar, grapefruit rind and 1 cup/250 ml/8 fl oz juice in a non-reactive saucepan and cook, stirring, over a low heat until sugar dissolves.

2. Combine sugar syrup, wine and remaining juice, pour into an ice cream maker and freeze following manufacturer's instructions.

3. Alternately, pour mixture into a shallow freezerproof container and freeze until ice crystals start to form around the edges. Using a fork, stir to break up ice crystals. Repeat the process once more then freeze until firm.

ingredients

> 1 cup/250 g/8 oz sugar
> 1 tablespoon finely grated ruby grapefruit rind
> 4 cups/1 liter/1 3/4 pt ruby grapefruit juice
> 1/2 cup/125 ml/4 fl oz champagne or sparkling wine

....

Serves 8

tip from the chef

Serve sorbet in scoops with slices of peach or nectarine.

watermelon
sorbet

■□□ | Cooking time: 15 minutes - Preparation time: 10 minutes

ingredients

> ²/₃ cup/170 g/5¹/₂ oz sugar
> 1¹/₄ cups/300 ml/10 fl oz water
> 2¹/₂ cups/625 ml/1¹/₄ pt watermelon purée
> 2 egg whites

method

1. Place sugar and water in a saucepan and cook over a low heat, stirring, until sugar dissolves. Bring to the boil, reduce heat and simmer for 10 minutes. Remove from heat and set aside to cool.
2. Mix watermelon purée into sugar syrup, pour into a freezerproof container and freeze until almost solid.
3. Place in a food processor or blender and process until smooth. Beat egg whites until soft peaks form and fold into fruit mixture. Return to freezerproof container and freeze until solid.

Makes 1.2 liters/2 pt

tip from the chef

Try these tempting variations.
Mango and passion fruit sorbet: Replace watermelon purée with 2 cups/500 ml/16 fl oz of mango purée and pulp of 4 passion fruit.
Kiwifruit sorbet: Replace watermelon purée with 2 cups/500 ml/16 fl oz of kiwifruit purée, ¹/₄ cup/60 ml/2 fl oz freshly squeezed grapefruit juice and 2 tablespoons mint liqueur.

blueberry
champagne sorbet

■□□ | Cooking time: 15 minutes - Preparation time: 10 minutes

method

1. Combine sugar, champagne and water in a large saucepan over moderate heat. Bring to the boil, reduce heat and simmer for 10 minutes.
2. Blend or process blueberries with lemon juice until smooth. Add syrup (a), mix well; cool to room temperature.
3. Pour into a lamington tin, cover with foil and freeze for several hours or until partially set. Remove from freezer and break up any ice with a fork (b).
4. Beat egg whites with an electric mixer until soft peaks form, fold into blueberry ice (c) until combined. Return to freezer and serve when frozen.

ingredients

> 1¹/2 cups/360 g/12 oz caster sugar
> 1 cup/250 ml/8 fl oz champagne
> 2 cups water
> 2 small boxes blueberries
> ¹/2 cup/120 ml/4 fl oz freshly squeezed lemon juice
> 2 egg whites

....
Serves 8

tip from the chef

If using an ice-cream maker, process according to instructions.

a

b

c

pumpkin and pecan ice-cream

■□□ | Cooking time: 0 minute - Preparation time: 15 minutes

ingredients

- > **8 egg yolks**
- > **3/4 cup/185 g/6 oz caster sugar**
- > **1 1/2 cups cooked, mashed pumpkin**
- > **1 1/2 cups light cream, whipped**
- > **3 teaspoons vanilla essence**
- > **1 teaspoon ground cinnamon**
- > **1/2 teaspoon ground nutmeg**
- > **1 cup chopped pecan nuts**

method

1. Beat egg yolks with sugar until thick, pale and creamy. Fold in mashed pumpkin, whipped cream, vanilla essence, cinnamon and nutmeg.
2. Pour mixture into a loaf tin, cover with foil and freeze until partially set.
3. Remove from freezer, break up any ice with a fork, beat mixture with electric mixer until ice crystals are broken up. Return to freezer until partially set and repeat.
4. Fold pecan nuts into ice-cream; pour back into loaf tin, cover with foil and freeze until set.

....
Serves 8

tip from the chef

For the pecan nuts to be crunchier, dry them in the oven at low temperature for 10 minutes.

the perfect
pavlova

■ □ □ | Cooking time: 2 hours - Preparation time: 15 minutes

method

1. Place egg whites in a mixing bowl and beat until soft peaks form. Gradually add sugar, beating well after each addition (a), until mixture is thick and glossy. Fold cornflour and vinegar into egg white mixture (b).
2. Grease a baking tray and line with nonstick baking paper. Grease paper and dust lightly with flour. Mark a 23 cm/9 in diameter circle on paper.
3. Place one quarter of the egg white mixture in the center of the circle (c) and spread out to within 3 cm/1¼ in of the edge. Pile remaining mixture around edge of circle and neaten using a metal spatula or knife.
4. Bake at 120°C/250°F/Gas ½ for 1½-2 hours or until firm to touch. Turn off oven and cool pavlova in oven with door ajar. Decorate cold pavlova with cream and top with fruit.

....
Serves 8

ingredients

> **6 egg whites**
> **1½ cups/315 g/10 oz caster sugar**
> **6 teaspoons cornflour, sifted**
> **1½ teaspoons white vinegar**
> **315 ml/10 oz cream, whipped**
> **selection of fresh fruits (orange segments, sliced bananas, sliced peaches, passion fruit pulp, berries, sliced kiwi fruits)**

tip from the chef

Both Australia and New Zealand claim to have created this truly marvelous dessert. However, both agree that it is named after the famous Russian ballerina.

a

b

c

passion
fruit pavlova

■□□ | Cooking time: 1 1/2 hour - Preparation time: 15 minutes

ingredients

> **6 egg whites, at room temperature**
> **pinch of cream of tartar**
> **2 teaspoons cornflour**
> **1 cup/250 g/8 oz caster sugar**
> **1¹/2 cups light cream, whipped**
> **4 passion fruits**
> **1 tablespoon fresh mint, cut into fine strips**

method

1. Beat egg whites with a handheld electric mixer until glossy. Combine cream of tartar, cornflour and sugar and gradually add to egg whites while motor is operating. Continue to beat for a further 5 minutes.
2. Grease and line the base and sides of a 23 cm/9 in springform tin with baking paper and lightly dust with cornflour, shake off any excess. Spoon meringue into prepared tin and spread top with knife to even out.
3. Bake at 130°C/260°F/Gas 1 for 1¹/2 hours. Turn off oven, leave door ajar and leave meringue to cool for 30 minutes. When cool, top with whipped cream, passion fruit and mint.

....

Serves 6-8

tip from the chef

Another option for topping the pavlova is to mix the whipped cream with raspberry purée and decorate with red fruits.

lemon
cheesecake

■ □ □ | Cooking time: 0 minute - Preparation time: 15 minutes

method

1. Place jelly crystals and gelatin in a bowl, pour over water and mix to dissolve. Cool to room temperature.
2. Place yogurt and cottage cheese in a food processor or blender and process until smooth. Add jelly mixture and process until combined.
3. Beat egg whites until soft peaks form, gently fold into cheese mixture. Pour mixture in a 20 cm/8 in springform tin, lined with plastic food wrap. Refrigerate until set.
4. Arrange strawberries on top of cheesecake. Garnish with blackberries on top and fresh mint sprigs around the base.

ingredients

- > 3 tablespoons lemon jelly crystals
- > 1 tablespoon gelatin
- > 1 cup/250 ml/8 fl oz boiling water
- > 2/3 cup/140 g/4 1/2 oz low-fat natural yogurt
- > 1 cup/250 ml/8 fl oz low-fat cottage cheese
- > 2 egg whites
- > 120 g/4 oz strawberries, hulled and halved
- > blackberries, to garnish
- > fresh mint sprigs, to garnish

....

Serves 6

tip from the chef

Dissolve a little extra lemon jelly crystals in hot water, cool to room temperature and drizzle over strawberries.

index